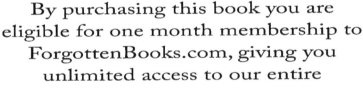

ISBN 978-0-656-05842-6
PIBN 10495485

BOSTON PLATE AND WINDOW GLASS CO.

FACTORY AND OFFICE

261 TO 267 A STREET, BOSTON

MANUFACTURERS AND JOBBERS

WINDOW GLASS, PLATE GLASS, MIRRORS

FRAMED MIRRORS AND PICTURE GLASS OF SELECTED QUALITY

SHOW ROOMS

20 AND 22 CANAL STREET, BOSTON

TO THE TRADE

WE herewith hand you our Mirror Catalog of 1913-1914 and by careful inspection of its pages you will find that it contains a

Line of Framed Mirrors

that is certainly very attractive. Both the Frames and Mirrors are from carefully selected stock and we do the silvering by a process which has stood the test of many years and is the equal of any process used here or abroad.

In presenting this catalog, we have been careful to select only such designs as will appeal to the artistic public, and to the conservative trade. It being impossible to incorporate in it every style that we carry—75 numbers, but on request, our salesman will call on you with full line of photographs.

Prices will be quoted on application, all inquiries being carefully and promptly handled. All goods are f. o. b. Boston.

We are not responsible for breakage or damages of any nature. Our responsibility ceases when goods are delivered in good order to the different transportation companies. We will say in this matter that goods are packed extremely well by men of experience in packing this line of goods.

For convenience of our trade, we have an entire line of these frames on exhibition at our show rooms, Nos. 20 and 22 Canal Street, Boston.

BOSTON PLATE & WINDOW GLASS CO.

287 A Street, Boston, Mass.

Polished Oak Frames

Fitted with Plate Glass Mirrors and Shocks as per List Shown Below

Superior Finish   Every Frame Paper Backed

Sizes	Width of Frame	American (Shocks)	Plain French	Bevel French
6 x 8	1 inch	$0.17	$0.34	$0.52
7 x 9	1 "	.20	.46	.60
8 x 10	1½ "	.26	.62	.86
9 x 12	1½ "	.32	.82	1.16
10 x 14	1½ "	.40	1.00	1.84
10 x 17	1½ "	.50	1.25	1.85
12 x 18	1½ "	.65	1.80	2.10
12 x 20	2 "	.70	1.90	2.30
14 x 24	2 "	.94	2.50	3.10
16 x 20	2 "		2.60	3.20
16 x 28	2½ "		3.75	4.80
18 x 32	3 "		4.75	5.50
18 x 40	3 "		6.75	7.50
20 x 24	3 "		4.26	4.80
22 x 28	3 "		5.50	6.00
24 x 30	3 "		9.80	7.50

oak frames, and can now offer you a finish superior to anything on the market.

No. 500	No. 505
A five piece combination gilt, made for the best premium trade.	A five piece combination gilt, made for the best premium trade.

Sizes
18x40, Plain . . . . . **$8.60**   Beveled **$9.60**
14x24, "   . . . . . **4.00**   " **4.55**

Sizes
18x40, Plain . . . . . **$8.60**   Beveled **$9.60**
14x24, "   . . . . . **4.00**   " **4.55**

No. 1303

Genuine mahogany, gold leaf frame, a beautiful oval, finished in gold leaf exceedingly attractive, built along the lines of the French Empire mirror. Size about 18x40.

Price $56.00

No. 1801

Reproduction of the Sheraton design with ornament finished with genuine gold leaf, eagle top, finished throughout with genuine mahogany, dowelled points, size about 12x20, fitted with plain French plate mirror.

Price $26.00

Constant application of business methods have made our line one of stability.

No. 1302

A reproduction of the Sheraton design, patterned after the old master's design, with ornament finished with genuine gold leaf, urn top, finished throughout with genuine mahogany, dowelled points, size about 12x20, fitted with plain French plate mirror.

Price **$26.00**

No. 1304

Old Colonial style of Washingtonian period, gold leaf burnishes throughout, genuine mahogany, American eagle top, fitted with French plate mirror. A reproduction of mirror frame now at the White House. Size 14x28.

Price **$62.00**

Attractive frames at low prices always on hand.

No. 525

This is made in all wood, no composition. About 4 inches wide, finished in all gilt. The smooth parts on the scroll ornaments are gold burnished, with burnish line on inner edge.

Sizes

16x28, Plain . . . . $ 7.00   Beveled . . . . $ 8.30
18x40, " . . . . 10.50   " 11.50

No. 550

Finished in either Rosewood or Circassion. Very highly polished. An artistic frame for finest art trade.

Sizes

16x20, Plain	$ 4.90	Beveled . (Rosewood)	$ 5.45
16x20, "	4.90	" . (Circassion)	5.45
18x40, "	11.25	" . (Rosewood)	12.25
18x40, "	10.90	" . (Circassion)	11.90

Then Quality Always Our Motto.

No. **555**

No. **540**

No. **545**

This is one of the best sellers on the market and especially suitable for mirrors. It is heavily burnished and the outside ornament blends well making it an attractive frame throughout. Finished in all gilt. This would make a good addition to your line.

Very handsomely ornamented and profusely burnished. Finished in all gilt and gold burnish.

Finished in all gilt and heavily burnished ornaments with dainty connecting ornament. Very popular pattern with furniture trade.

Size
14x24, Plain . . $7.00 Beveled . . . $7.70

Size
11x24, Plain . . $4.50 Beveled . . . $5.05

Size
14x24, Plain . . $4.85 Beveled . . . $5.40

Our process of resilvering will make an old mirror almost as good as new. But will not take out scratches.

No. 802

A 4 inch antique frame made of special compo with dull bronze showing our new Grecian type, size 16x20, fitted with plate glass mirror.

Plain . . . . $3.85   Beveled $4.05

No. 811

16x20 frame especially adapted for mirrors, is a 2 inch oval gilt with a handsome inside bead ornament near the front edge which throws off the plain gilt background. Reasonable in price and each frame packed separately in shadow boxes.

Plain . . . . $3.55   Beveled $4.05

Mirrors finished with polished edges and rounded corners.

No. 920

New circassian oval with burnishes around the entire outside edge of frame, making an attractive and pleasing design.

Size

18x40, Plain . . . . . **$12.00**   Beveled **$13.00**

No. 845

Oval gilt 4 inches wide, inside gold stripe with full ornaments. One of our best frames and a ready seller.

Size

18x40, Plain . . . . . **$11.50**   Beveled **$12.50**

If prompt and efficient service mean anything we should secure your business.

No. 916

Dresden finish frame of the French period, handsome effect, with plain French plate mirror. This frame is certainly a work of art, and one that will bear your closest attention.

Size
12x24, Plain . . . . . $7.25   Beveled $7.75

No. 966

Dresden finish frame, hand colored, marked with very distinctive lines, an up-to-date pattern in every respect.

Size
18x28, Plain . . . . . $9.25   Beveled $10.00

This is a mirror catalogue of course. We carry everything that can be found in a first class jobbing house dealing in glass alone.

Boston Plate & Window Glass Co.

No. 905	No. 955	No. 1203	No. 1204
Two opening French antique mirror frame, fitted with old English prints of varied assortment, fitted with French plate glass mirror, size 5⅜x20. Entire outside measurement of this frame would be about 8x32½ inches.	Dresden finished frame of antique design, artistic top ornament, fitted with imported print, size 10x14. This magnificent frame measures over all 14x54 inches. It is hand colored throughout, attractive and ornamental. Size of plate 10x34, plain	A dainty, hand carved, antique mirror frame, outside measurement about 8½x32 inches, fitted with a hand colored Christy photo, size 6x8. with a plain French plate glass mirror, size 6x20.	A dainty, hand carved, antique mirror frame, outside measurement about 8x30. This is almost the same design as our No. 1203 only showing a new color head of Christy's latest work.
Plain . $3.00 Beveled . $3.30	Price $8.25	Price $4.50	Price $4.40

The tea trade will find in this catalogue a number of framed mirrors just suited for premiums.

No. 1201

New pastel frame, hand colored Dresden finish throughout; this season's latest novelty in art frames, a two opening frame with imported French print, size 6x8. Mirror will measure 5⅜x20. Outside measurement of frame about 6x32.

Plain **$4.25**

No. 1202

The same as our No. 1201 pattern with the slight exception that this has the wreath ornament on top making a very pleasing effect. A two opening frame with imported French print, size 6x8. Mirror will measure 5⅜x20. Outside measurement of frame about 6x32.

Price **$4.24**

No. 1200

Circassian mirror frame, outside measurement about 14x52, fitted with an Imported French print, size 10x14, hand colored of the famous Emperor Napoleon. Size of mirror 10x34. The corners of this frame are finished with dull bronze gold ornaments. An exceedingly handsome frame.

Price **$9.00**

No. 817

Antique French mirror frame finished in gold and bronze, outside of frame about 14x 54, fitted with colored French print, size 10x14; French plate glass mirror size 10x34.

Price **$7.75**

All sizes of polished plate glass mirrors, excellent quality, can be furnished at short notice.

No. 750

Bronze frame, highly ornamented, about $2\frac{1}{2}$ inches wide, artistic corners, frame suitable for parlor or boudoir.

Size
18x24, Plain . . . . . **$7.60**   Beveled **$8.20**

No. 755

Artistic circassian frame, with a series of gold ornaments. This season's latest pattern, a staple frame and one that will give entire satisfaction.

Size
18x40, Plain . . . . . **$9.60**   Beveled **$10.60**

If you do not find what you want in this catalogue send for one of our salesmen; he will assist you.

No. **880**

Dainty full burnished mantel top mirror frame, finished in bronze and gilt, latest design.

Size

1¼x24, Plain . . . . . $7.25   Beveled $7.80

No. **938**

A square gilt frame, full sweep, inside gold combination frame, made to sell at a popular price.

Size

18x40, Plain . . . . . $14.50   Beveled $15.50

Permit us to pick out a sample line.

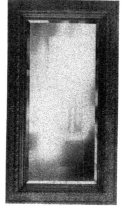

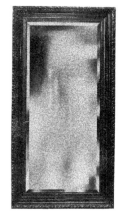

No. 930

3 inch square circassian, made of full stock and burnished on all corners.

Size

18x40, Plain . **$10.00**   Beveled . **$11.50**

No. 562

5 inch combination frame, new pattern, all gilt of excellent quality, frame that will make a good showing in any line, moderate in price. Quality and a leader.

Size

18x40, Plain . **$8.50**   Beveled . . **$9.50**

No. 935

Gilt mirror, inside gold finish, 5 inches wide; deep border of heavy bronze; very attractive frame.

Size

18x40, Plain . **$14.00**   Beveled . **$15.00**

We make a specialty of an assorted case containing six framed mirrors all new patterns. Try a sample case. **Price on application.**

No. 618

No. 620

This is one of the new designs in ovals, very dainty, neat ornaments richly burnished connecting wreath ornament, a big seller.

A combination double decker with outside member plain. This shows off the stem which is carved, bored and cornered. It looks nice in all gilt with plenty of burnishes.

Size

Size

18x40, Plain . . . . . **$10.50**   Beveled **$11.50**

18x40, Plain . . . . . **$10.90**   Beveled **$11.90**

No order however small but will receive best attention.

No. **825**

A new oval with bow-knot ornamentation. Full stock, 4 inches wide, all gilt and burnished.

Size

18x40, Plain . **$10.50**   Beveled . : **$11.50**

No. **830**

One of the seasons latest designs in oval shape with 24 burnishes in bronze and gilt. A very elaborate frame.

Size

18x40, Plain . **$10.50**   Beveled . . **$12.30**

No. **865**

At a popular price, this oval is the best on the market. 4 inches wide, outside ornaments of gold bead and made in lacquered bronze finish. A high class frame at a low price.

Size

18x40, Plain . **$10.00**   Beveled . . **$11.00**

The show rooms at our 20 Canal Street office are convenient to the trade.   Salesmen always there to show you the line.

No. 937

The latest model square frame, tapestry effect, four inches wide.

Size
10x40, Plain . **$11.50**   Beveled . . **$12.50**

No. 627

The very latest 6 corner oval made. Very richly designed and massive ornaments heavily burnished with dainty connecting strap. Do not fail to get this in your line as it is a LEADER.

Size
18x40, Plain . **$12.20**   Beveled . . **$13.20**

No. 640

A new double deck frame nearly 7 inches wide, handsomely ornamented corners and sides and neat ornamental back setting off the stem. Finished in gilt, full gold burnish, this size only.

Size
18x40, Plain · **$13.40**   Beveled · · **$15.30**

Our goods give satisfaction. Give us a trial order.

No. 623

No. 625

All gilt oval of excellent finish and burnish. Artistic and fully ornamented; a frame of merit.

A handsome new 4 inch oval in early English polished walnut effect, large pearl, full burnish setting of the walnut finish. One of the handsomest ovals ever made and a great seller.

Size
18x40, Plain . . . . . **$10.90**   Beveled **$11.90**

Size
18x40, Plain . . . . . **$12.20**   Beveled **$13.20**

When in our city we should be pleased to have you accept the courtesy of our show rooms.

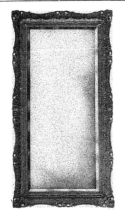 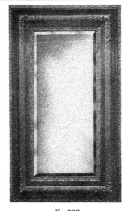 

No. 608	No. 603	No. 610

No. 608

A new double decker, richly modeled, very low price, bound to be a great seller; handsomely ornamented, hand laid corner ornaments.

Size

18x40, Plain . **$8.60**   Beveled . . **$9.60**

No. 603

This is a very popular combination frame with ornamented wide outside reeded stem, plain inside and gilt lining, corners heavily burnished, 7 inches wide.

Size

18x40, Plain . **$11.00**   Beveled . **$12.00**

No. 610

A new 3 inch sweep frame, heavy ornaments bored and carved, one large ball burnished on corners and centers.

Sizes

16x20, Plain . **$ 4.20** Beveled . . **$ 4.75**

18x40,   "   .   **9.30**   "   . . **10.30**

We crate and pack all goods in solid cases—it saves breakage.

No. **850**

Heavy double deck oval, with massive ornament and full burnished; one of the best patterns to be had at the price.

Size
18x40, Plain, ... **$16.50**   Beveled **$17.50**

No. **970**

Oval gilt mirror frame, ornamented top and bottom, 8½ to 4 inches wide, genuine hand gilt work on this frame.

Size
18x40, Plain . . . . . **$15.00**   Beveled **$16.00**

The illustrations on this page do not do these mirrors justice. **Must be seen to be appreciated.**

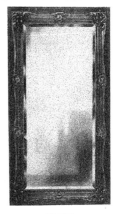

No. 855

Upright mirror frame of staple pattern, used as a Pier or mantel mirror. Carried in the following sizes:

18x36, Plain . **$10.00**   Beveled . **$11.00**
18x40,   "   .   11.00   "   .   12.00

No. 601

Something new, the latest and best 4 inch composition frame yet produced, finished in all gilt. Lot of frame for little money.

Size

18x40, Plain . **$8.40**   Beveled .   **$9.40**

No. 925

A new circassion, 36 gold burnishes, 4 inch wide with full sweep, all gilt stem.

Size

18x40, Plain . **$12.25**   Beveled . **$13.25**

Table tops and dressers are now being covered with plate glass. We make them in any size.

  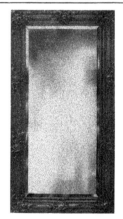

No. 900

Wide gilt frame made with a shell sweep and ornamented back, 4 inches wide, very handsome pattern.

Size
18x40, Plain . **$11.50**   Beveled . . **$12.50**

No. 835

Full four-inch sweep, gold frame, raised stem, with full ornaments and 24 burnishes of bronze and gilt.   Very effective design.

Size
18x40, Plain . **$11.30**   Beveled . . **$12.30**

No. 920

Gilt frame, artistic design and the season's best seller, made in all gold finish, highly ornamented gold burnishes throughout.

Size
18x40, Plain . **$10.50**   Beveled . . **$11.50**

Oval mirror frames are always acceptable for new homes.   Our line is varied and large.

No. 812

A new frame of antique design with a strong touch of the old Empire in it. Made of solid wood throughout, with excellent gilt and bronze effect. Sizes as follows carried in stock.

14x24, Plain . . . . . $ 6.00   Beveled . . . . $ 6.50
18x36,   "   . . . . . 11.25   " 12.25
18x40,   "   . . . . . 12.50   " 13.50

No. 612

A 4 inch oval with heavily burnished ornaments with connecting strap.

Size
18x40, Plain . . . . . $9.80   Beveled $10.80

We are importers of Sharratt & Newth's Glaziers' Diamonds.

No. **645**   **Mantel Top Mirror**

Size 18x50, Ends, 12x18, Center 18x24

Considered one of the best three opening frames on the market. The ornaments are neat and attractive, setting off the dainty shape design.

Plain . . . . **$12.40**   Beveled **$14.00**

No. **870**

4 inch oval, full gilt, highly ornamented, new pattern.

Size

18x40, Plain . . . . . **$9.75**   Beveled **$10.75**

Every frame in this catalogue has been selected with great care, all material being of the best to be had at a moderate price.

No. **650**

Illustrates this season's latest design in mantel with massive top ornament and connecting wreath, colonial style heavily gold burnished. Best selling number in the line and can be had upright or mantel.

Plain . . . . **$12.20**   Beveled **$13.20**

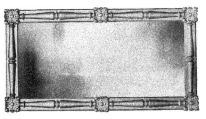

No. **809**

Beautiful old Colonial frame. Simplicity is the key-note of this number. Made of the best turned stock with a fine dull bronze finish.

Size
18x40, Plain . . . . . **$15.75**   Beveled **$16.70**

Colonial and Old Empire mirrors are selected with great care, the work being done by an experienced artist.

White Enameled Square Frames

Of Excellent Quality, Each Packed in a Separate
Box and Paper Backed

Size of Glass	Width of Frame	Price of Plain Framed Mirror White Enamel	Price of Beveled Framed Mirror White Enamel
8x10	1 inch	$ .70	$ .95
9x12	1 "	.85	1.20
10x14	1½ "	1.20	1.55
10x17	1½ "	1.70	2.10
12x18	1½ "	2.10	2.50
12x20	2 "	2.50	3.00
16x20	2 "	3.35	3.90
18x22	2 "	2.85	3.35
14x24	2 "	3.50	4.05
16x24	2 "	4.00	4.60
16x28	3 "	5.25	6.00
18x30	3 "	6.00	6.75
18x36	3 "	7.20	8.10
18x40	3 "	8.00	9.00

LIBERAL DISCOUNTS TO THE TRADE

All Sizes on Above Carried in Stock; Can Furnish any
Quantity on Short Notice

Plate glass shelves mak

Plate Glass Shelves

Edges Polished and Corners Rounded

Heavy Plate Glass of Full 1-4 inch Stock Used Only

Size	Price Each	Price Doz.
5x18	$ .78	$ 8.75
5x20	.77	9 25
5x22	.81	9.75
5x24	.84	10.00
5x26	.96	11.50
5x28	1.00	12.00
5x30	1.04	12.50

Above Prices Include Nickle on Brass Brackets

DISCOUNT ON APPLICATION

Nickel Framed Mirrors

NO DUST

CAN

GATHER

ON THEM:

MOISTURE PROOF

No. 1002   Plain, Square Corners

Size of Mirror	Long Price Plain	Long Price Beveled
16x20	$5.10	$5.70
16x24	6.25	6.80
18x24	7.40	8.00

No. 1003   Plain Oval

Size of Mirror	Long Price Plain	Long Price Beveled
12x20	$4.00	$4.50
16x20	4.60	5.10
16x24	5.60	6.25
18x24	6.75	7.25

They look and keep clean all the time.

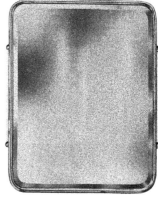

Nickel Framed
Mirrors

———

JUST THE

BEST KIND

OF

FRAMED MIRRORS

FOR

BATH ROOMS

No. 1000 **Beaded and Round Corners**

Size of Mirror	Long Price Plain	Long Price Beveled
12x20	8 7.00	8 7.50
16x20	8.25	8.75
16x24	9.75	10.25
18x24	10.50	11.25

Nickel plated frames made of brass and be

No. 1001 **Plain With Round Corners**

Size of Mirror	Long Price Plain	Long Price Beveled
12x20	$4.50	$5.00
16x20	5.50	6.00
16x24	7.00	7.50
18x24	7.75	8.50

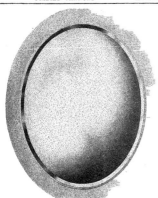

White Emamel
Frames
Our Own
Special Finish

**THE FINISH
ON THESE FRAMES
IS OF THE BEST.
AS TIME AND
EXPERIENCE
HAVE PROVED IT.**

725

Size of Glass	Width of Frame		Price of Plain Framed Mirror White Enamel	Price of Beveled Framed Mirror White Enamel
12x18	1½	inch	$ 2 75	$ 3.20
12x18	2	"	2 80	3.25
12x20	2	"	3 00	3 45
16x20	1½	"	3 60	4.15
16x20	2	"	3.65	4.20
14x24	1½	"	3.80	4.40
14x24	2	"	3.95	4.50
16x24	1½	"	4.25	4.90
16x24	2	"	4.45	5.10
18x40	3	"	10.50	11.50

710

Size of Glass	Width of Frame		Price of Plain Framed Mirror White Enamel	Price of Beveled Framed Mirror White Enamel
12x18	1½ inch		$2.80	$3.25
12x20	2	"	3 05	3.50
10x20	1½	"	3.75	4.25
16x20	2	"	3.85	4.40
14x24	1½	"	3.95	4 50
14x24	2	"	4.10	4.70
18x24	1½	"	4 45	5.10
16x24	2	"	4 05	5.25

We specialize on bath room mirrors.

Sanitary Frameless Bath Room Mirrors

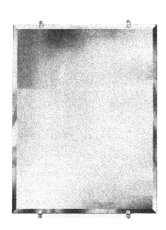

The most sanitary and modern bath room fixture on the market; made from the best French Mirror Plate, with edges polished square and chamfered and back coated to make the mirror impervious to moisture; furnished with our PATENTED ADJUSTABLE CLIPS, with nickel-plated Screws—no dust can gather on back. The following list of sizes are to be had in stock at any time:—

10x17	$2.30
12x20	3.00
14x24	4.00
16x28	5.50
18x24	5.00
18x40	8.75
20x24	5.50
22x28	7.25
24x30	8.60

Each Mirror Packed Complete in Neat Paper Carton

For the picture trade our extra selected paper packed picture glass compares favorably with any brand on the market.

Lightning Source UK Ltd.
Milton Keynes UK
UKHW011636231118
332794UK00013B/2088/P